Fun with Shapes

FUN WITH TRIANGLES

Bert Wilberforce

PowerKiDS press

New York

Let's look for triangles!

triangle

The chip looks like a triangle.

The cheese looks like a triangle.

The sandwich looks like a triangle.

The ruler looks
like a triangle.

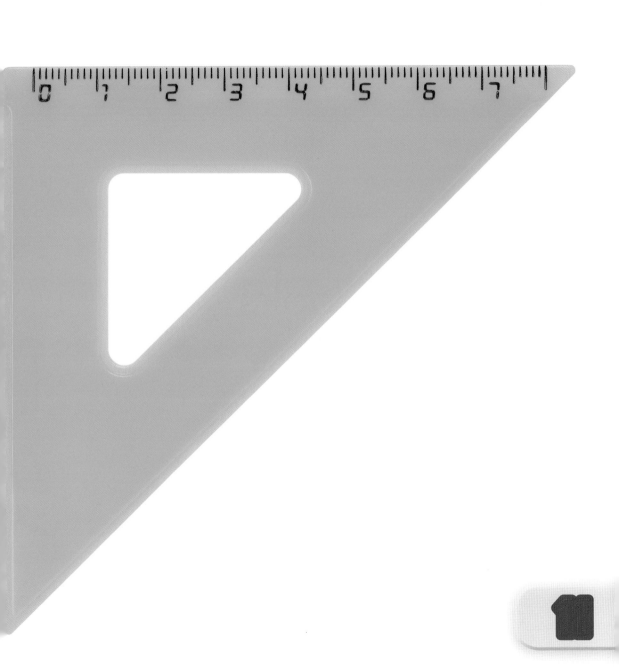

The flag looks
like a triangle.

The napkin looks like a triangle.

The pillow looks like a triangle.

The bowl looks like a triangle.

19

The watermelon looks like a triangle.

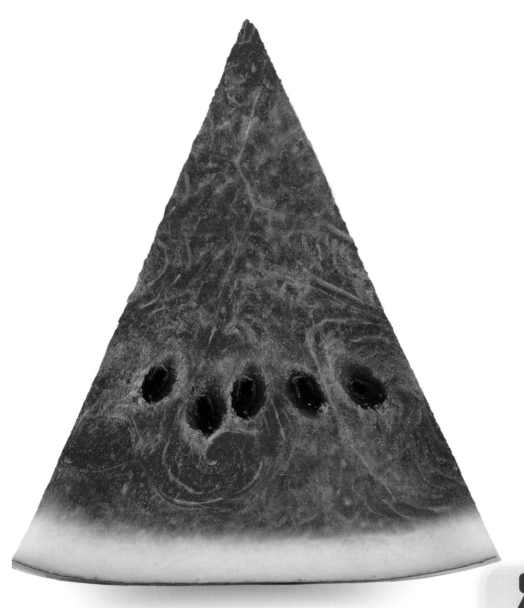

Do you see triangles?

Published in 2023 by The Rosen Publishing Group, Inc.
29 East 21st Street, New York, NY 10010

Copyright © 2023 by The Rosen Publishing Group, Inc.

First Edition

Editor: Therese Shea
Book Design: Rachel Rising

Photo Credits: Cover, p.1 Stoker_Studio/Shutterstock.com; p. 3 Sylwia Brataniec/Shutterstock.com; p. 5 xpixel/Shutterstock.com; p. 7 D_M/Shutterstock.com; p. 9 stock-enjoy/Shutterstock.com; p. 11 Tatiana Popova/Shutterstock.com; p. 13 TerraceStudio/Shutterstock.com; p. 15 Eshma/Shutterstock.com; p. 17 Arctos/Shutterstock.com; p. 19 tim08/Shutterstock.com; p. 21 Superheang168/Shutterstock.com; p. 23 Michael J P/Shutterstock.com.

Library of Congress Cataloging-in-Publication Data

Names: Wilberforce, Bert, author.
Title: Fun with triangles / Bert Wilberforce.
Description: New York : PowerKids Press, [2023] | Series: Fun with shapes
Identifiers: LCCN 2021046326 (print) | LCCN 2021046327 (ebook) | ISBN
  9781538385593 (library binding) | ISBN 9781538385579 (paperback) | ISBN
  9781538385586 (set) | ISBN 9781538385609 (ebook)
Subjects: LCSH: Triangle--Juvenile literature.
Classification: LCC QA482 .W587 2023 (print) | LCC QA482 (ebook) | DDC
  516/.154--dc23/eng/20211117
LC record available at https://lccn.loc.gov/2021046326
LC ebook record available at https://lccn.loc.gov/2021046327
Manufactured in the United States of America

Some of the images in this book illustrate individuals who are models. The depictions do not imply actual situations or events.

CPSIA Compliance Information: Batch #CSPK23. For further information contact Rosen Publishing, New York, New York at 1-800-237-9932.

Find us on